Colors of the Earth
By Ronnie Townsend

The ocean shines blue in many places all over the world. Do you see blue?

The leaves on trees scream with green. Do you see green?

The flowers are filled with many rich shades of pink. Do you see pink?

The color white beams through many waterfalls and streams. Do you see white?

Soil covers the ground with brown. Do you see brown?

The canyons of the desert beam with orange, do you see orange?

Peppers are not only delicious to eat, but they come in many colors and one of those colors happens to be red. Do you see red?

The night sky is reunited every evening with the color black. Do you see black?

Many rocks in the forest are known for being grey. Can you see the color grey?

When driving on the road, there are two yellow lines. Do you see yellow?

The tomatoes have just started sprouting and they are a light green. Do you see green?

The flowers are a beautiful shade of yellow and they are facing every direction. Do you see yellow?

There are many purple flowers covering the forest floor. Do you see purple?

Among many green trees, there is a pink tree that stands out. Do you see pink?

When the sun sets, it lights up the horizon with the glow of orange. Do you see orange?

On days when the sky isn't blue, it sometimes can be a smooth grey. Do you see grey?

In nature, berries can be found in many colors and some even in the color red. Do you see red?

As I look out onto the river, there are many soft white flowers. Do you see white?

Sunflowers are filled with yellow and have a way of brightening up the day. Do you see yellow?

There are many different colored peppers, and green peppers are sure delicious. Do you see green?

The horse has a long and beautiful black mane.
Do you see black?

There are times when more than one color can be seen in the evening skyline as the sun sets. How many colors do you see?

There are many colors of the world, and colors make the world go round. Colors such as red, yellow, grey, and brown. The world is a rainbow, and every color of that rainbow is waiting to be seen.